# The Thr
# Wi

Written by Maire Buonocore
Illustrated by Ray Mutimer

Collins *Educational*
An imprint of HarperCollins *Publishers*

# Characters

1 The narrator

2 The farmer

3 The farmer's wife

4 The gnome

**Narrator:** *A farmer was walking in the forest. He met a gnome, whose foot was stuck in a hole.*

**Gnome:** Hey! You! My foot is stuck in this hole. Get me out!

**Farmer:** All right. I'll pull you out.

**Gnome:** Ow! Be careful! Ouch!

**Narrator:** *The farmer pulled and pulled, until at last... pop! The gnome's foot suddenly shot out of the hole and the farmer and the gnome fell over.*

**Gnome:** Look what you've done! My boot is still in the hole. Humans are so silly!

**Farmer:** That's not fair. We're not silly.

**Gnome:** Yes, you are. I can prove it. I'll give you and your wife three wishes. You will be sure to waste them. That's how silly humans are.

**Farmer:** We're not silly, and we won't waste them.

**Narrator:** *The gnome followed the farmer home and hid behind the door.*

**Gnome:** This will be fun! Let's see what these silly humans do now.

**Wife:** You're very late today.

**Farmer:** Yes. I'm sorry. You see, I met a gnome in the forest... and his foot was stuck in a hole.

**Wife:** A gnome stuck in a hole?

**Farmer:** Yes. I helped him. So he granted us three wishes...

**Wife:** There you go again, making up stories. Come on. Sit down and have your tea. We're having eggs. The hens laid lots of eggs today.

**Farmer:** Oh no! Not eggs again! I'm fed up with eggs. I wish we could have a great big jam roly-poly.

**Gnome:** Ha! Ha! A jam roly-poly! That is your first wish gone.

**Narrator:** *At that moment, a great big sticky jam roly-poly appeared on the table.*

**Wife:** Well, that was a waste of a wish, wasn't it? How could you be so stupid? We could have wished for anything.

**Farmer:** I'm sorry, I didn't think.

**Wife:** You never do, do you? Look at that silly jam roly-poly! I wish it were stuck on the end of your nose!

**Gnome:** That's the second wish gone!

**Narrator:** *At that moment, the jam roly-poly jumped up and stuck on the end of the farmer's nose.*

**Wife:** Oh no! What have I done?

**Farmer:** Look at my nose!

**Wife:** I'm sorry, I didn't think.

**Farmer:** What shall we do? We can't leave it there.

**Wife:** Why not? It doesn't look too bad.

**Farmer:** No, it must come off.

**Narrator:** *The wife tugged at the roly-poly, but it would not come off.*

**Farmer:** Ow! Be careful! Ouch!

**Wife:** I think there is only one way to get it off.

**Farmer:** You're right.

**Both:** We wish the jam roly-poly were back on the dish.

**Gnome:** That's the third wish gone!

**Narrator:** *At that moment, the jam roly-poly jumped back on to the dish.*

**Wife:** Now let's eat our eggs.

**Farmer:** And our jam roly-poly.

**Narrator:** *So the farmer and his wife ate their tea, and the gnome went back to the forest to find his boot.*

**Gnome:** I knew humans were silly!